Music for Flute & Piano

INTERMEDIATE LEVEL
Volume 3

CONTENTS

To access audio visit:
www.halleonard.com/mylibrary

Enter Code
1863-3311-9108-4356

ISBN 978-1-59615-303-5

Music Minus One

EXCLUSIVELY DISTRIBUTED BY

Hal•Leonard®

7777 W. BLUEMOUND RD. P.O. BOX 13819 MILWAUKEE, WI 53213

Visit Hal Leonard Online at
www.halleonard.com

PERFORMANCE GUIDE
COMMENTARY BY DONALD PECK

MOZART
Andante in C Major, K. 315

Although this Andante is most often performed separately, it was written as an alternate movement for the Concerto in G Major, K 313. You will need to be careful of the rests. They should not be stopping places; the musical thought must flow right through! The articulation will be too percussive if you use a "t" syllable; use the "duh-guh" when you need to double-tongue a passage.

The trill in the opening measure of the flute part may be played like this:

You will probably get a better sounding trill in measure 86 if you lift the index finger of the left hand slightly. (If you lift it too high, the sound may be too open.)

These trills should all be gracious and light. Heavy, dramatic trills would be out of character. You can make a trill at the end of a phrase more important by putting it on the beat.

Editor's Note: Mr. Peck has supplied his own Cadenza, which follows.

LANE
Sonata: 1st Movement, Allegro vivace

This piece is in typical sonata-form. There is a first theme, a second theme, and then both themes are worked out together in a development section. Try to contrast the moods of the first and second themes. The first theme can be tight and intense; the second theme can be more open and *dolce*. When you reach the development, you can bring out the interplay of these two themes by changing tone quality accordingly. The development reaches its climax in measure 46. After a recapitulation of the first two themes, there is a coda beginning in measure 67. An understanding of the structure will make this music much more interesting.

The trill in measure 19 is very awkward. If you trill with both the index finger and the thumb, you will get a better sound. This trill will need extra practice! You can use regular fingering in measure 44.

There is a group of five sixteenth notes in the second theme. If you think of this group as a combination of three and two you will get a more placid feeling. (If the same group occurred in the first theme, a combination of two and three would make a more brilliant effect.)

You will need to anticipate the entrances on sixteenth notes. If you wait until you hear the piano, react, and then get your flute to speak, you may be too late. Notice the two fragments of the first theme in measure 28. A fragment of the second theme occurs in measure 30, and an inversion of the second theme begins in measure 35. Work for clarity so that your audience can appreciate all of the composer's devices!

GLUCK
Minuet and Dance of the Spirits from "Orfeo"

This is an arrangement of ballet music from the opera, Orfeo. A study of the libretto might help you to interpret this piece more interestingly. The Minuet is quite placid, with pathos and yearning. Notice the crescendos and decrescendos in the Dance. The dynamics must not be overdone. Play expressively, but never romantically. You can vary your intensity and vibrato for dynamic contrast. The grace notes should have melodic value. Do not let the rests stop the flow of music. If you continue your thought through the rests, they will give the music a sense of urgency and flow.

ANDERSEN
Scherzino, Op. 55, No. 6

This piece is in typical Scherzo form: two fast sections with a Trio in the middle and a Coda at the end. It should have a playful mood. There are not many places to breathe, so you will have to pace yourself carefully. Keep the piece moving freely. It must never sound stiff or studied. Do not sustain the trills in the first section too long; you have to leap down a whole octave after them, and the low notes take time to speak. It is common practice to play the Trios of Scherzos a little more relaxed than the rest of the piece. Play the grace notes lightly, and not too fast. The mood of the Trio is *dolce,* and the ornaments must always match the mood!

HANDEL
Sonata No. 3: Adagio and Allegro

Don't play this Adagio too slowly. Handel Adagios have a certain characteristic nobility which may be lost if the tempo doesn't have enough flow. There must always be a forward movement. Ornaments should not be played quickly. Fast trills sound too romantic for the Handel style. They should be played before the beat, and measured evenly. Be sure your vibrato is narrow. This music does not need a "juicy" tone. Work for a concentrated tone with core and point.

The Allegro should be quite brilliant with many "terraced" dynamic levels. There are many opportunities for echo effects, and you should be aware of the interchange between the solo part and the accompaniment. Think ahead to the ritard at the end. It must be decisive and final. You may insert a trill in the final cadence if you wish.

Donald Peck

ANDANTE IN C, K. 315

WOLFGANG A. MOZART
Edited by Himie Voxman

Cadenza by Tillmetz

SONATA

♩ = 82 (2'57")
♩ = 76 (3'25")

RICHARD LANE

MINUET AND DANCE
OF THE BLESSED SPIRITS

♩ = 66 (5'21")

C. W. von GLUCK

Menuet

Lento dolcissimo

Spirit Dance

Più lento (in 6)

SCHERZINO

JOACHIM ANDERSEN
Op. 55, No. 6

SONATA NO. 3 IN G MAJOR

♩=82 (1'37")

G. F. HANDEL